WHAT'S THE **BIG IDEA?**

POLITICS
and
DEMOCRACY

Tim Cooke

Cavendish Square

New York

Published in 2018 by Cavendish Square Publishing, LLC
243 5th Avenue, Suite 136 New York, NY 10016

© 2018 Brown Bear Books Ltd

Website: cavendishsq.com

CPSIA compliance information: Batch #CS17CSQ:

All websites were available and accurate when this book went to press.

Library of Congress Cataloging-in-Publication Data

Names: Cooke, Tim.
Title: Politics and democracy / Tim Cooke.
Description: New York : Cavendish Square, 2018. | Series: What's the big idea?: a history of the ideas that shape our world | Includes index.
Identifiers: ISBN 9781502628145 (library bound) | ISBN 9781502628152 (ebook)
Subjects: LCSH: Political science--Juvenile literature. | Democracy--Juvenile literature. | State, The--Juvenile literature.
Classification: LCC JA70.C66 2018 | DDC 321.8--dc23

For Brown Bear Books Ltd:
Managing Editor: Tim Cooke
Editorial Director: Lindsey Lowe
Designer: Supriya Sahai
Design Manager: Keith Davis
Children's Publisher: Anne O'Daly
Picture Manager: Sophie Mortimer

Manufactured in the United States of America

CONTENTS

INTRODUCTION

In the Western world, people are familiar with democracy. They vote to elect people who then govern the country on their behalf.

The earliest societies were probably ruled by groups of elders. These were the most experienced and wisest members of the group. By around 3000 BCE, however, kings and emperors ruled their subjects as **absolute monarchs**. Citizens gained the right to vote on government decisions in Athens and Rome in the 500s and 400s BCE. However, Rome later gave power to absolute emperors. After the fall of Rome in 476 CE, Europe was ruled by kings who claimed to rule with the support of God.

This painting shows citizens celebrating the creation of a **republic** in the French city of Metz in 1189. The republic gave the citizens the right to govern themselves.

Financial markets can operate across national borders. That weakens the authority of individual countries. How can democracy cope with such challenges?

From the 1200s onward, monarchs gradually gave up their absolute power. They granted rights to their nobles in return for their support, such as the right to a fair trial. Monarchs began to meet with groups of leading citizens, who gave the monarch advice. Later, these groups became elected bodies known as **parliaments**. Suffrage, or the right to vote, was originally limited to wealthy male citizens. Throughout the 1800s suffrage was extended first to all adult males and then in the early 1900s to women.

Threats to democracy

Although the emergence of democracy may have seemed inevitable, it was not. Even now, a third of the world's population lives under an **authoritarian** government. Such governments demand complete loyalty from their citizens, who have no personal freedoms. Meanwhile, the world's democracies face challenges that are very difficult to overcome. In some ways, democracy remains a fragile system of government.

WHAT IS DEMOCRACY?

Most experts believe the form of government known as democracy has its roots in ancient Greece.

In a democracy, citizens govern their own country through elected representatives who take part in the government. The word "democracy" comes from the Greek words *demos*, meaning people, and *kratos*, meaning rule. Most people in the Western world live in democracies—and yet democracy is difficult to define.

ACROPOLIS

Ancient Greeks met to vote at the Pnyx, an open space on the Acropolis, a rocky hill overlooking Athens. →

A new political system

In simple terms, in a democracy political power lies in the hands of the citizens. The people exercise that power by voting for the good of all the people. Exactly who is entitled to vote, however, has varied widely. For much of history, monarchs ruled their lands without consulting their subjects. Parliaments were introduced in Europe from around the 1200s. The first voters were usually wealthy male property owners. During the 1800s, working men were given the vote. Women only gained the vote comparatively recently. Children have never been able to vote, but the age at which people can vote varies in different countries.

The right to vote raises many **moral** questions. Should people in prison be allowed to vote? Should voting be mandatory, as it is in Australia? And is it more democratic for people to elect representatives or to make direct choices between options? This latter process is known as a referendum.

TIMELINE

500s BCE Solon introduces a type of democracy in Athens, although government is dominated by the **aristocratic** elite.

509 BCE Citizens of Rome in Italy overthrow their king and found a republic. The republic begins a period of expansion across Italy and around the Mediterranean.

27 BCE Augustus becomes the first emperor of Rome. The emperors continue to expand the empire before it enters a long period of decline.

Around 2,500 years ago, what is now Greece was divided into many small **city-states**. In the early 500s BCE, Solon, the ruler of Athens, introduced an assembly that included all male citizens. However, the assembly could only vote on decisions taken by the aristocratic **magistrates** who still held real political power. Late in the 500s, an Athenian named Cleisthenes introduced further changes that reduced the power of the aristocracy. The changes included allowing other more ordinary citizens to hold office.

Limited democracy

Despite further reforms in the 400s BCE, few Athenians were actually entitled to vote. Foreigners, slaves, and women were excluded, and male citizens had to have completed their military training. In practice, only between 10 and 15 percent of Athenians were allowed to vote.

BANISHED

Athenians voted to banish citizens from Athens by scratching the person's name on a broken piece of pottery, known as an ostracon.

LAWGIVER

Solon's role in introducing democracy to Athens earned him the nickname "the Lawgiver." He intended his reforms to halt what he saw as a decline in Athenian morals. →

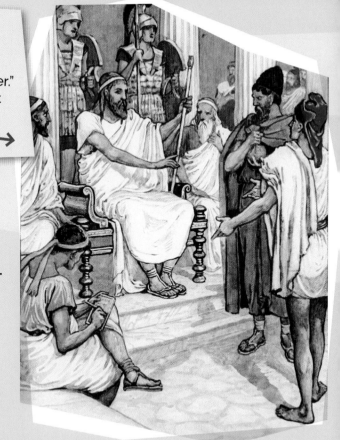

The Athenians met 40 times a year to vote on laws. They voted by a show of hands. Votes on whether to banish someone from Athens were made by secret ballot.

Ancient roots

The Athenians might not have been the first people to live in a democratic system. Historians believe that early **hunter-gatherers**, who could not read or write, may also have practiced an earlier form of democracy.

ATHENIAN GOVERNMENT

The government of ancient Athens had four main branches, each open to the four social classes into which all Athenian society was divided.

1. **Ecclesia (Assembly)—all male citizens:** made laws, elected officials
2. **Boule of 400—from top three classes:** proposed new laws and other decisions for the Ecclesia
3. **Archons (Magistrates)—from top two classes:** held senior government posts
4. **Areopagus (retired Archons)—**ensured the Ecclesia did not make illegal decisions

Early hunter-gatherers may have made decisions together in order to benefit the whole group. Later, when tribes started to live in settled communities, new kinds of political organization emerged. Individuals emerged as chiefs or kings, and the majority of people lost their say in decisions.

The ancient Romans

In 509 BCE, the people of Rome in Italy overthrew their ruler and created a republic. The word comes from the Latin words *res*, meaning "thing," and *publicus*, meaning "public." A republic was "a thing belonging to the people."

Rome was a city-state. Its citizens met at the Forum, a large open space surrounded by important government buildings. Each year the people elected two consuls to be the chief officials.

FORUM

Romans voted at the Forum either in an assembly of all citizens, known as a committee, or a specific class of citizens, called a council.

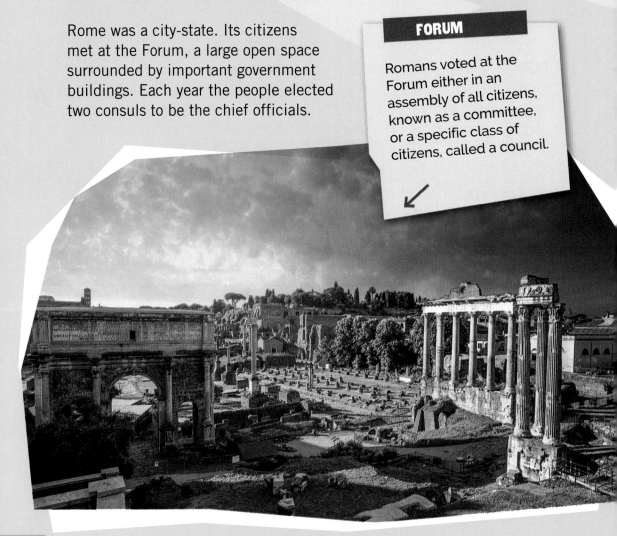

SENATE

The Senate brought together Rome's leading aristocrats to debate new laws. Senators had power over many decisions made by the Roman government. →

They also elected judges, tax collectors, and tribunes who looked after the poor. The consuls received advice from the Senate, a body of about 600 leading citizens who helped make Rome's laws.

Senators were not elected. Most came from old, aristocratic families. However, other Romans put up with them because the Senate helped Rome to expand its power over Europe, North Africa, and parts of the Middle East. Rome became so wealthy that ambitious politicians no longer wanted to serve as elected consuls. In 44 BCE, Senators murdered the politician Julius Caesar for saying that Rome should become a one-ruler state. In 27 BCE, Augustus became the first emperor of Rome, ending the republic.

IN SUMMARY

■ Democracy is widely seen as having had its roots in ancient Athens in the 500s and 400s BCE.

■ In Athens and in the Roman republic, democracy was limited. Only wealthy citizens could vote. The traditional elite had more power in government than the voters.

THE AGE OF MONARCHY

Rome's emperors were absolute rulers. Absolute rulers had existed for thousands of years.

The pharaohs had ruled Egypt from around 3500 BCE. They were absolute rulers, with complete power over their subjects. Rome's emperors also had unlimited power. Unpopular emperors, however, might be killed by their enemies, or even by their own armies.

EMPEROR

Charlemagne kneels before Pope Leo III. The pope made Charlemagne Holy Roman emperor in 800.

PIPINVS REX

Monarchy and religion

In 313 CE, the Roman Emperor Constantine converted to Christianity. Christianity became the official religion of the empire in 380. Constantine's conversion changed the relationship between politics and religion. It helped make Rome the center of the Catholic Church, ruled by the pope. Christianity played a vital role in how Europe developed after the Roman Empire in the West was overthrown by Germanic peoples in 476.

The fall of Rome began a period that is sometimes known as the "Dark Ages." Roman rule had united Europe under the same government, but that unity was now replaced by many small kingdoms and states. Their kings or leaders fought each other constantly for land. Then, in 800, the pope crowned Charlemagne, king of the Franks, as Holy Roman emperor. Charlemagne temporarily unified much of Europe under his rule. After his death, the continent again split into small kingdoms.

TIMELINE

476 The Roman Empire in the West is overthrown by Germanic peoples. This begins the "Dark Ages."

800 Charlemagne is made Holy Roman emperor by Pope Leo III. This helps to forge a strong link between the church and monarchy in Europe.

1206 Genghis Khan unites all the Mongol tribes under his rule. He begins to build a vast empire stretching from China to eastern Europe.

ꟼPHANVS P P

After Charlemagne, the support of the pope and the Catholic Church became essential to rulers trying to establish their authority. Some nobles claimed that they were more entitled to rule than other nobles because they had the support of the church. Europe was highly religious, and the Catholic Church provided religious authority throughout the continent. If the church supported a king, it showed that God had appointed him. It was the duty of the king's subjects to obey him. As royal **dynasties** became more established, the king's authority to rule became seen as a "divine right," given by God.

A support structure

Most kings relied on supporters who could fight well. In order to gain and keep their support, the king granted them land and titles. This helped to create a **hereditary** aristocracy in countries such as England and France. These warrior barons fought on behalf of their rulers in frequent wars. In most of Europe, military power became the most important way of keeping power.

EMPEROR

The Frankish king Charlemagne ruled much of central Europe. He helped to spread Christian learning. →

The Doge of Venice

A different system operated in the city-states of Venice and Genoa. Venice and Genoa were successful ports that traded in goods from as far away as China. The leading citizens of these states elected a ruler. He was named the "doge," from the Latin word *dux*, meaning a military leader. The doge served for life, but over time his powers over those he ruled became severely limited.

VENICE

The doge was an elected ruler, but real power over the Venetian republic lay in the hands of the aristocrats who elected him.

THE RISE OF MONARCHIES

Powerful monarchies emerged around the world in the Middle Ages (ca. 500–ca. 1500).

Europe
Holy Roman Emperor

Mongolia/China
Mongol Emperor

Turkey
Ottoman Emperor

Cambodia
Khmer Emperor

Andes
Inca Emperor

Istanbul
Byzantine Emperor

Around the world

It was not only in Europe that military success was the basis of political power. In southeast Asia, the Khmer people had defeated their neighbors to establish an empire that covered what are now Cambodia, Thailand, and Laos. The Khmer Empire was at the height of its powers between 802 and 1431. The Khmer king ruled as an absolute monarch from Angkor in Cambodia.

The Mongols came from the mountains of eastern Mongolia. They were expert horsemen. Beginning under the military leadership of the **warlord** Genghis Khan in the late 1100s, the Mongols expanded their territory. In a period of around 170 years, the Mongols used military skill to conquer China and Korea in the east. In the west their armies defeated Persia (modern Iraq) and reached Russia and Poland.

On the other side of the world, the Inca Empire of Peru was the largest empire in pre-Columbian America.

CONQUEROR

Genghis Khan advanced into China and eastern Europe. His descendant Kublai Khan further expanded the Mongol empire.

The Inca began to conquer their neighbors and increase their territory in the 1200s. Like the Khmer and the Mongols, the Inca used violence to control their enemies. They were ruled by an absolute ruler, the Sapa Inca. The Inca reached the height of their power in the 1500s, shortly before they were overthrown by a small force of invading Spaniards.

Obedience and Protection

By the late Middle Ages, individuals in much of the world had few rights. They had little or no say in how they were ruled. They were expected to show obedience and **allegiance** to a king. In exchange, they could expect their king's protection against their enemies.

IN SUMMARY

- The rule of absolute monarchs spread in the Middle Ages, helped by a close connection between kings and the Catholic Church.

- Strong kings and emperors came to power in different societies around the world.

KINGS AND PARLIAMENTS

In the later Middle Ages, kings found their authority limited. Nobles wanted more power for themselves. This led to new forms of government.

One of the earliest and most influential attempts to limit a monarch's power came in England in 1215. The English king, John, was unpopular because he taxed his subjects heavily to pay for wars he was fighting to gain power in France. A group of John's leading nobles, or barons, threatened not to pay. They forced him to sign a peace treaty. The treaty is known as the Magna Carta, or "great charter."

MAGNA CARTA

King John relied on the support of his barons, so he signed this charter agreeing to limit his power over his subjects. →

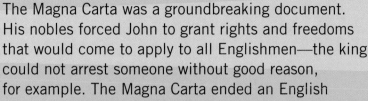

The Magna Carta was a groundbreaking document. His nobles forced John to grant rights and freedoms that would come to apply to all Englishmen—the king could not arrest someone without good reason, for example. The Magna Carta ended an English monarch's right to absolute rule.

It also started a movement that would transform European politics. The rights the nobles demanded would filter down to all members of society over the next centuries.

Parliament

From the 1260s, English nobles refused to cooperate with kings who acted alone and did not call a parliament if they wanted to raise taxes and hire soldiers. This parliament was an assembly of nobles and wealthy citizens. It was a place for people to talk (from the French word *parler*, meaning "to talk"). Parliament could challenge or block the king's plans.

TIMELINE

1215 King John I of England signs the Magna Carta, giving his barons and other English citizens basic rights.

1649 English Parliamentarians execute King Charles I during the English Civil War. It is a clear sign that people no longer believe in the divine right of kings.

1789 The French Revolution breaks out. The revolutionaries overthrow the monarchy and create a republic, although it will only last until 1804.

The English parliament grew stronger over the following centuries. In the 1500s, the **Reformation** began when the Protestant Church challenged the authority of the Catholic Church in Europe. There were religious wars throughout Europe. Monarchs who defended the authority of the pope fought against those rulers who saw Protestantism as a means to increase their own royal power. In 1533, the English King Henry VIII broke with the Roman Catholic Church when the pope refused to allow him to divorce his wife, Catherine of Aragon. Henry made Protestantism the state religion in England. He granted the English parliament more powers in return for its support.

The English parliament

In 1642, English Parliamentarians went to war against King Charles I. The rebels claimed that the king could not impose taxes on them without their consent. The Civil War ended in victory for Parliament in 1651. In 1649, during the war, the Parliamentarians had beheaded King Charles I. It was a sign the monarchy was no longer "divine."

PARLIAMENT

Queen Elizabeth I of England opens Parliament in 1586. In the 1500s, the English monarch summoned Parliament to ask its advice on questions of government. →

EXECUTION

Parliamentarians execute King Charles I on January 30, 1649. In 1629, Charles had decided to rule without consulting Parliament, a decision that led to civil war.

←

England became a republic until Charles's son was invited to restore the monarchy in 1660. Despite the Restoration, the English monarch could no longer rule without the consent of parliament. The message was reinforced in 1688, when the members of parliament removed King James II and gave his throne to the Dutch prince William of Orange.

Parliament was now at the heart of English government. It had two chambers: the House of Lords and the House of Commons. Nobles sat in the House of Lords by right of their birth. The House of Commons was for non-noble Members of Parliament elected by citizens with the right to vote.

LIMITING THE POWER OF KINGS

Over a period of about 570 years, various peoples used warfare or rebellion to weaken or destroy the absolute power of their rulers.

England **1215**
KING JOHN I

England **1649**
KING CHARLES I

American colonies **1765**
KING GEORGE III

France **1789**
KING LOUIS XVI

Across the English Channel

Things were different in continental Europe. In France, the monarchy still had absolute authority. Although the French parliament, called the Estates General, had met in 1614, it did not meet again until 175 years later. Instead, French kings such as Louis XIV, who ruled from 1643 until 1715, increased the power of the monarch. None of the king's subjects had a chance to influence the king's decisions, from the nobility to the peasants. This rigid form of absolute rule eventually led to the overthrow of the French monarchy.

Revolution!

Meanwhile, England faced an unexpected challenge from its American colonies. Colonists were increasingly angry toward the English parliament. Parliament was taxing the colonies, although no colonists were allowed to vote. "No taxation without representation" became the rallying cry for protests that eventually led to the Revolutionary War (1775–1783). With support from France, American patriots defeated the British Army.

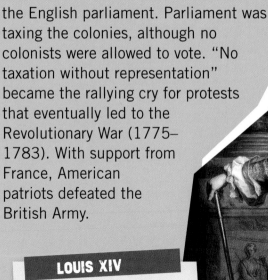

LOUIS XIV

Louis XIV was known as the "Sun King." He raised the status of France both through warfare and by making his court at Versailles the center of Europe's fashionable life. →

SURRENDER

The British general Lord Cornwallis surrenders to U.S. forces at the Battle of Yorktown in 1781. Defeat forced Britain to accept U.S. independence.

In France, the excesses of absolute rule became clear when King Louis XVI left the state nearly bankrupt by the mid-1780s. At the same time, French nobles inspired by the Revolutionary War in America wanted more political power. Ordinary French people, meanwhile, were angry at rising prices and the introduction of higher taxes. On June 17, 1789, the French created a new parliament, the National Assembly. It was the first step toward the French Revolution. The monarchy did not survive.

IN SUMMARY

- Monarchs gradually gave up their absolute powers in return for the support of their nobles, partly in order to be able to raise money.

- The idea of a king's divine right was ended by anti-monarchy movements in England, North America, and France.

EXTENDING THE VOTE

In the 1800s, ordinary people began to take part in politics through elections. However, there were still many restrictions on who had the right to vote.

The American and French revolutions had both been based on the idea of destroying a social **hierarchy** in which kings and nobles had a natural right to rule their subjects. The U.S. Declaration of Independence stated in 1776 that "All men are created equal." In 1789, the French Revolutionary Assembly declared "Men are born and remain free and equal in rights."

PARLIAMENT

The Palace of Westminster in London was built in the 1800s to house both parts of the British Parliament: the House of Commons and the House of Lords.

The U.S. **Constitution** of 1787 is the world's oldest written constitution. It set out the duties of government and its responsibilities to its citizens. In 1791, Congress passed the Bill of Rights. These 10 amendments to the Constitution guaranteed citizens certain rights. However, the Bill of Rights applied mainly to white males. It granted no specific rights to American women, Native Americans, or African Americans.

The United States

In France, the equality promised by the revolution lasted only briefly. In 1804 Napoleon Bonaparte declared himself emperor, bringing back the monarchy to France. In the United States, however, the republic continued to evolve its form of government. In the early 1800s the right to vote was limited to white men who owned property or paid taxes. This was named Jeffersonian Democracy for U.S. President Thomas Jefferson. Jefferson believed political power should lie mainly with the states. The voters who elected officials should come from an educated elite.

TIMELINE

1828	Andrew Jackson founds what is called Jacksonian democracy in the United States, based on a broad electorate.
1832	The Great Reform Act in Britain marks the first of a series of steps that expanded suffrage to virtually all adult male voters.
1920	Women gain the vote in the United States, following a protest campaign by suffragists and women's work for the war effort in World War I.

The restrictions on who could vote changed when states gave all white males over the age of 21 the right to vote. In the late 1820s, President Andrew Jackson introduced what is known as Jacksonian Democracy. In this program, virtually all white men were allowed to vote. Jackson increased the power of the president and federal government, giving them powers that had previously belonged to the individual states.

American women had no political representation, despite Iroquois women having had equal voting rights in their tribes from as early as 1654. The new territory of Wyoming gave women the vote in 1869. The right for most women to vote in national elections only came with the Nineteenth Amendment in 1920.

Britain and its Empire

In Great Britain, suffrage became an important political issue in the 1800s. Parliament passed a series of three separate reform acts in 1832, 1867, and 1884. The acts extended the right to vote for adult males. As late as 1918, however, only 58 percent of British men could vote.

JACKSON

Andrew Jackson was president from 1829 to 1837. He set out to expand the U.S. electorate to include nearly all adult white males by abolishing requirements that voters own property.

A system of conditions excluded many from voting. Military personnel serving overseas, for example, were excluded by a requirement that all voters had to have lived in Britain for a period of 12 months before any election.

British women still could not vote. Angered by their exclusion, a group of women formed the Suffragette Movement in 1867. For the next 50 years they held demonstrations and raised **petitions** to try to force the government to grant them the vote. The dispute became increasingly violent and bitter.

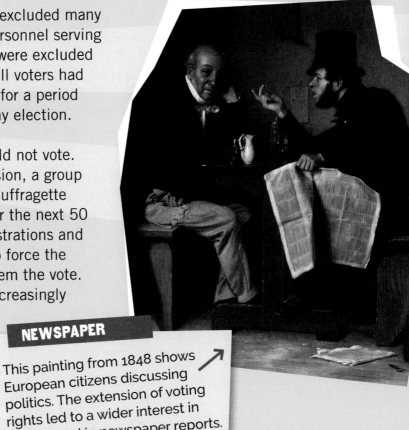

NEWSPAPER

This painting from 1848 shows European citizens discussing politics. The extension of voting rights led to a wider interest in politics and in newspaper reports.

VOTES FOR WOMEN

These are the dates when some countries gave women the right to vote in national elections. Women could vote in many local elections before these dates.

1840	Kingdom of Hawaii
1893	New Zealand
1902	Australia
1906	Finland
1918	Great Britain
1919	Netherlands
1920	United States
1931	Spain
1944	France

British suffragettes—known as suffragists in the United States—deliberately staged stunts to gain publicity. However, it was the important role that women played in the workplace in World War I (1914–1918) that eventually persuaded politicians to give women over the age of 30 the vote. Two years later, in 1920, American suffragists won the right to vote. As in Britain, the change in the law reflected the value of female contributions to the war effort.

Some of Britain's colonies were ahead of Britain in giving women equal voting rights with men. British colonies such as Canada, Australia, and New Zealand had introduced their own governments modeled on that of Britain. In the British colony of New Zealand, women had been able to vote since 1893.

PROTEST

U.S. suffragists drive in a parade in Washington, DC, in 1910. Their car is covered in American flags as a sign of their patriotism. →

African American civil rights protestors march from Selma to Montgomery in Alabama in 1965. They wanted voting rights for African Americans. ↑

Civil rights

African Americans remained largely excluded from voting. After the Civil War (1861–1865), the Fifteenth Amendment made it illegal to prevent black people from voting. However, several states introduced laws to get round this. The laws remained in place until the civil rights campaign of the late 1950s and early 1960s. The right for African Americans to vote was finally confirmed in the Civil Rights Act of 1965.

IN SUMMARY

■ The right to vote in elections was initially restricted to those who owned property. That restriction was relaxed throughout the 1800s.

■ Voting rights for women took longer to achieve, and those for African Americans took even longer.

POLITICAL THEORIES

In the 1800s and 1900s, new political theories emerged to challenge the idea that democracy was the best form of government.

One theory was **anarchy**, which is based on the idea that society can govern itself more fairly without any formal government or laws. The theory has its roots in the ideas of ancient Greeks such as Diogenes and Crates. In 1840, the Frenchman Pierre-Joseph Proudhon began the modern

KARL MARX

Marx spent much of his career in England, as his political ideas were not welcome in Germany.

anarchist movement when he published his book *What is Property?* Proudhon's answer to his own question was "Property is theft." Ideas such as the belief that private property was unjust made Proudhon influential, but anarchy was not successful as a political system. In the 1910s and 1920s anarchists launched terrorist attacks in the United States, but they made little impact.

The Industrial Revolution

A more influential political theory was **socialism**, which emerged in the mid-1800s. Thanks to the Industrial Revolution, more people left the land to work in factories in cities and towns. There was a growing difference between workers and their employers. The German socialist Karl Marx decided that the two groups had nothing in common. The **capitalist** system favored the employers. Marx argued that capitalism must be overthrown so that wealth could be redistributed among the workers.

TIMELINE

1848 Marx and Engels publish *The Communist Manifesto*. It is widely banned and makes little impact.

1917 Vladimir Lenin leads a revolution in Russia. It becomes the world's first communist country, with ideas based on the theories of Karl Marx.

1933 Adolf Hitler becomes chancellor of Germany. He makes himself dictator, outlawing all political opposition to the fascist policies of his Nazi Party.

Marx and his friend Friedrich Engels published *The Communist Manifesto* in 1848. They argued that workers must overthrow capitalism in a violent revolution. This idea was controversial, because it meant the overthrow of governments and rulers. The book was widely banned. However, in the 1870s similar ideas became popular in Europe. Social-democratic parties were formed with the aim of improving conditions for working people.

Communism

The theory of socialism was based on the idea of centralized control of economic activity. Marx's own philosophy, or "Marxism," was the basis of a more radical theory, known as "communism." Under communism, the community owns everything. Individuals contribute and are rewarded according to their ability.

In 1917, the Russian people revolted against their absolute monarch, Czar Nicholas II. A communist party known as the Bolsheviks seized power.

REVOLUTION

Bolshevik guards protect political leaders during the Russian Revolution in 1917. The Bolsheviks withdrew from World War I in order to fight a civil war in Russia.

←

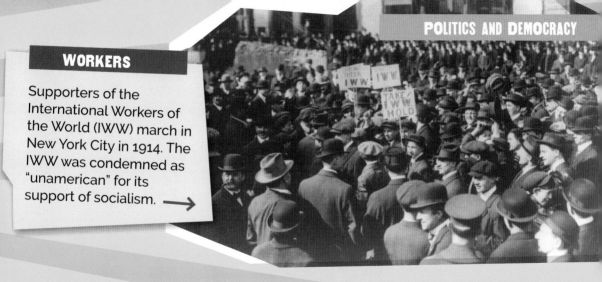

WORKERS

Supporters of the International Workers of the World (IWW) march in New York City in 1914. The IWW was condemned as "unamerican" for its support of socialism. ➝

Led by Vladimir Lenin, the Bolsheviks set out to establish a state based on the "dictatorship of the proletariat [industrial workers]." The former Russian Empire became the Soviet Union. Although many workers' councils were set up to make decisions about everyday life, the system was not democratic. The leaders of the Communist Party ruled as virtual **dictators**. After World War II, communism spread to Eastern Europe and into China and other Asian countries. Communism remained influential for four decades, but its failure to achieve economic growth ultimately led to the widespread collapse of communist states in 1989.

INDUSTRIAL WORKFORCE 1850

Marx's theory of communism was based on the increased number of workers in industry. These graphs show the percentage of industrial workers in 1850.

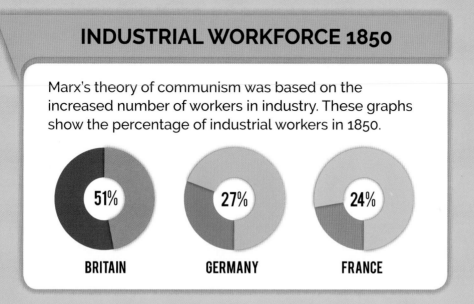

51% **BRITAIN**

27% **GERMANY**

24% **FRANCE**

Fascism

World War I left much of Europe in ruins. A new political ideology began to emerge. This was **fascism**. In many ways, it resembled Soviet communism. It put power in the hands of dictators. Individuals had few rights, and the state suppressed all opposition. Fascism was also highly **nationalistic**, but this was based on the **militarization** of society.

Fascism emerged in Italy in the 1920s. Italy had only been a country since 1861 and did not have a long tradition of democracy. Benito Mussolini was elected as prime minister in 1922. In 1925 he made himself dictator and outlawed political opposition. Mussolini promised to build a "fascist" state. The word comes from *fasces*, a bundle of rods tied together in ancient Rome as a symbol of strength through togetherness. Italians were attracted to Mussolini's promise of security.

Germany was another relatively new democracy. Adolf Hitler came to power there in 1933, and soon made himself dictator.

MUSSOLINI

The Italian leader Benito Mussolini (center) used fascism to appeal to Italians' desire to recapture the glories of ancient Rome.

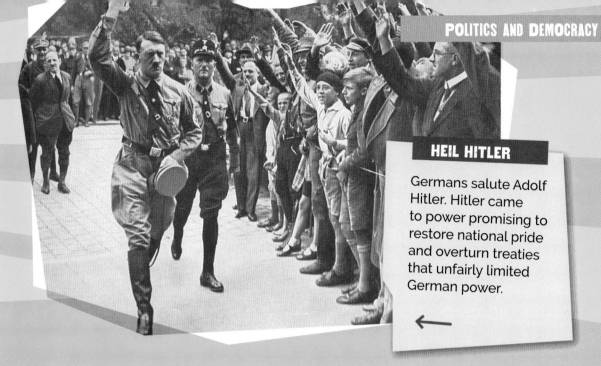

HEIL HITLER

Germans salute Adolf Hitler. Hitler came to power promising to restore national pride and overturn treaties that unfairly limited German power.

←

Hitler set up a fascist state that promised Germans an aggressive foreign policy in return for state control and a loss of personal freedom. Hitler's ambitions to expand Germany eventually led to World War II (1939–1945).

Even after the defeat of Germany and Italy in the war, fascism survived as a political theory. Dictators ruled Spain and Portugal in the second half of the 1900s, as well as numerous states in Africa, Asia, and South America. Few of these regimes lasted for a significant period, however.

IN SUMMARY

■ Communism was a reaction to industrial society in the 1800s. Many people feared its threat to outlaw private property.

■ Fascism emerged in the 1920s and 1930s. It resembled Soviet communism in many ways and led to World War II.

DEMOCRACY IN THE DIGITAL AGE

Although democracy is now the world's leading political system, many people still live in political systems that give them no say in how they are governed.

At the start of the 2000s, democracy was the world's dominant political system. There are 196 countries in the world. In 2013, 123 of them were democracies, and over half the global population lived in a democracy. A third of people still lived under an authoritarian leader, however. There were different degrees of democracy. Some countries held elections where only one party could have candidates, for example. Other democracies did not allow all their citizens to vote.

WARFARE

U.S. soldiers on patrol. Western forces fought terrorist groups in Afghanistan, Iraq, and elsewhere in the early 2000s.

→

The rise of ideology

In the early 2000s, the influence of democracy came under threat. Religious **ideology**, new technology, and **globalization** all threatened democratic institutions.

One of the most serious threats came from religion. Some Muslims, or followers of Islam, wanted to establish a religious Islamic state, known as a caliphate. A caliphate is a type of government called a theocracy. The word comes from the Greek words *theos*, or "god," and *kratein*, meaning "to rule." In a theocracy, the monarch or government claims to rule on behalf of a god or deity.

The first theocracy emerged in ancient Egypt 5,000 years ago. The pharaohs claimed they ruled Egypt on behalf of the gods. There have been many theocratic governments since, including the Vatican in Rome, which is governed according to Christian laws. The most recent attempt to establish an Islamic theocracy came in the Middle East.

TIMELINE

1989 British scientist Tim Berners Lee invents the World Wide Web, allowing communication between computers.

2012 The Occupy movement holds protests in countries around the world. They fight against globalization and the lack of accountability of corporations.

2014 The terrorist group ISIS seizes territory in Syria and Iraq as part of an attempt to create an Islamic caliphate in the Middle East.

A terrorist group calling itself Islamic State (ISIS) seized large areas of land in Syria and Iraq in 2014. Its ambition was to set up a caliphate that crossed national borders, within which everyone would follow an extreme form of Islam. It appealed to a sense of injustice about how Western countries have treated Muslims throughout history, although most of its victims were fellow Muslims. In 2016, armed forces in the Middle East began to drive ISIS from its strongholds. However, governments in the region have become more authoritarian and less democratic as they try to resist the threat from the group.

New technology

ISIS gained supporters by using social media. More generally, new technology such as computers, smartphones, and tablets, has allowed people to connect across national borders, time zones, and language barriers. Ideas and information are transmitted instantly around the world.

DESERTS

The threat from Islamist terrorism comes mainly from the Middle East, where governments lack the power or the will to control terror groups. ↓

ELECTION

A dyed finger shows this man has voted in Afghanistan's first direct election, held in 2009. The West introduced elections after defeating the country's extremist Islamic rulers.

←

On the one hand, technology allows more citizens to engage in political debate more easily. This seems like a benefit for democracy, as it encourages voters to participate. On the other hand, critics fear that the Internet also encourages unmoderated or extremist opinions. It is easy for half-truths or lies to become accepted as fact. Critics say that this undermines reasoned debate and that it puts government in the hands of an ill-informed mob.

MODERN THEOCRACIES

Seven countries are theocracies in the modern world, meaning their leaders are considered to have been given authority by God.

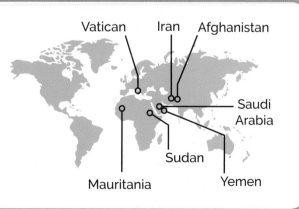

Vatican   Iran   Afghanistan

Saudi Arabia

Sudan

Mauritania

Yemen

Global corporations

Another challenge to modern democracy comes from globalization. Democracy has traditionally been linked with capitalism, in which people have the freedom to maximize their earning power. This approach is seen as having led to a rise in living standards since the end of World War II in 1945.

In a global world, however, corporations are less subject to national laws. They can move their operations to suit themselves. They can also cut their bills by paying taxes in countries with low tax rates rather than in countries where they earn their income. Voters of individual countries have less power to restrict economic activities of which they disapprove.

STOCK MARKET

Some people fear that international finance now has more influence than politics in the actions of governments around the world. ↓

↑ Young Canadians protest globalization in Toronto in 2012. The protest was part of an international movement known as Occupy.

In the 2010s, popular demonstrations broke out around the world. They were against global corporations acting as they wish. They also highlighted the apparent inability of democratic governments to stop the corporations. The future of democracy may depend on the ability of democratic powers to address the concerns raised by such protests.

IN SUMMARY

■ Democracy faces a number of challenges in the modern world. Democratic countries must evolve to meet them.

■ Voters in democracies have become frustrated over their lack of power to influence processes such as economic globalization.

THE WORLD TODAY

Today a third of the world's population still live under an authoritarian government. Most countries are democracies, however.

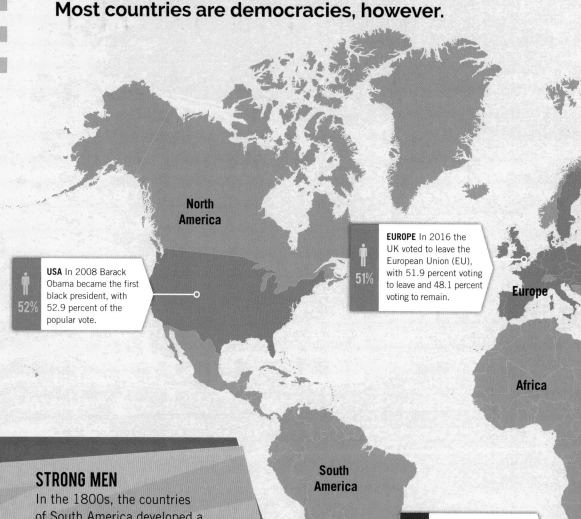

North America

USA In 2008 Barack Obama became the first black president, with 52.9 percent of the popular vote.

52%

EUROPE In 2016 the UK voted to leave the European Union (EU), with 51.9 percent voting to leave and 48.1 percent voting to remain.

51%

Europe

Africa

South America

STRONG MEN

In the 1800s, the countries of South America developed a tradition of "caudillos," or "strong men," who ran governments in an authoritarian way. In the 1900s the tradition was continued by a series of military governments in various countries.

SOUTH AFRICA Black and ethnic South Africans, who make up 91 percent of the population, only got the right to vote in 1994.

91%

FAILED STATES

In a failed state, a country's political or economic system is so weak that the government is no longer in control. Recent examples of this include war-torn countries such as Somalia, Sudan, and Syria.

Asia

CHINA China is run by the Communist Party. The Chinese (20 percent of the world population) have no right to vote.

20%

MYANMAR Myanmar was run by a military dictatorship until elections in 2015.

SAUDI ARABIA is an absolute monarchy. The king is free to rule as he sees fit.

FACTFILE:
THE WORLD'S MOST FULLY **DEMOCRATIC COUNTRIES** IN 2016 IN ORDER:

  Norway
  Iceland
  Sweden
  New Zealand
  Denmark
  Switzerland
  Canada
  Finland
  Australia
  Netherlands
  Luxembourg
  Ireland
  Germany
  Austria
  Malta

FACTFILE:
Five countries have communist governments:
  China
  Cuba
  Laos
  North Korea
  Vietnam

FACTFILE:
Libya in North Africa has not had a recognized government since the overthrow of the dictator Muammar Gaddafi in 2011.

TIMELINE

500s BCE
Solon introduces a type of democracy in Athens, although government is dominated by the aristocratic elite.

509 BCE
Citizens of Rome in Italy overthrow their king and found a republic. This begins a period of Roman expansion across Italy and then around the Mediterranean.

27 BCE
Augustus becomes the first emperor of Rome. The emperors continue to expand the empire before it enters a long period of decline.

476 CE
The Roman Empire in the West is overthrown by Germanic peoples. This begins the Dark Ages.

800
Charlemagne, king of the Franks, is made Holy Roman emperor by Pope Leo III. This helps to forge a strong link between the church and monarchy in Europe.

1206
Genghis Khan unites all the Mongol tribes under his rule. He begins to build a vast empire stretching from China to eastern Europe.

1215
King John I of England signs the Magna Carta, giving his barons and other English citizens basic rights.

1649
English Parliamentarians execute King Charles I during the English Civil War. It is a clear sign that people no longer believe in the divine right of kings.

1787
After U.S. independence, the U.S. Constitution becomes the first written constitution in the world.

1789
The French Revolution breaks out. The revolutionaries overthrow the monarchy and create a republic, although it will only last until 1804.

1828
Andrew Jackson founds what is known as Jacksonian democracy in the United States, based on a broad male electorate.

| 1832 | The Great Reform Act in Britain marks the first of a series of steps that expanded suffrage to virtually all adult male voters. |

| 1867 | The Women's Suffrage Movement begins in Britain. |

| 1870 | Following the Civil War, black Americans are granted the vote under the Fifteenth Amendment, but states throughout the South use Jim Crow laws to discriminate against African American voters. |

| 1917 | Vladimir Lenin leads a revolution in Russia, which becomes the world's first communist country based on the theories of Karl Marx. |

| 1920 | Women gain the vote in the United States, following a protest campaign by suffragists and a key contribution by women to World War I. |

| 1933 | Adolf Hitler becomes chancellor of Germany. He makes himself dictator, outlawing all political opposition to the fascist policies of the Nazi Party. |

| 1964 | African Americans receive the vote through the Civil Rights Act. |

| 1989 | British scientist Tim Berners Lee invents the World Wide Web, allowing communication between computers. |

| 2012 | The Occupy movement protests in countries around the world at globalization and the lack of accountability of multinational corporations. |

| 2014 | The terrorist group ISIS seizes territory in Syria and Iraq as part of an attempt to create an Islamic caliphate in the Middle East. |

GLOSSARY

absolute monarchs Rulers with no limits on their authority.

allegiance Loyalty or commitment to a superior.

anarchy A political ideal based on absolute personal freedom, with no government.

aristocratic Belonging to the aristocracy, the highest class in a society, made up of people of noble birth.

authoritarian Requiring strict obedience.

capitalist Connected with an economic system in which individuals are free to practice any legal economic activity.

city-states Self-governing political units comprising a city and its surrounding land.

constitution The set of fundamental ideas by which a country is governed.

dictators Rulers with total power.

dynasties Series of rulers who all come from the same family.

fascism An extreme right-wing system of government.

globalization The process by which businesses begin to operate on an international scale.

hereditary Passed on from parents to their offspring.

hierarchy A system in which people are ranked according to their importance.

hunter-gatherers Early peoples who lived by hunting animals and gathering fruits and other food.

ideology A system of ideas that forms the basis of a political theory.

magistrates Officials who act as judges in law courts.

militarization The process of organizing a society ready for military action.

moral Related to right or wrong, or good or bad behavior.

nationalistic Devoted to one's country.

parliaments Bodies of elected and other representatives that govern a country.

petitions Formal written requests to authority to act in a particular way.

Reformation The period from 1517 to 1648 when Protestantism challenged the Roman Catholic version of Christianity.

republic A state in which supreme power is held by citizens and their representatives.

socialism A political theory that says that government should regulate economic acitivty to make society fairer.

suffrage The right to vote.

warlord A regional military commander.

FURTHER RESOURCES

Books

Andrews, David. *Business Without Borders: Globalization.* The Global Marketplace. Chicago: Heinemann, 2010.

Bhote, Tehmina. *Charlemagne: The Life and Times of an Early Medieval Emperor.* New York: Rosen Publishing Group, 2005.

Cates, David. *Karl Marx: Philosopher and Revolutionary*. Essential Lives. Edina, MN: Abdo Publishing Company, 2011.

Gregory, Josh. *The French Revolution.* Cornerstones of Freedom. New York: Scholastic, 2013.

Hardyman, Robin. *What Is a Democracy?* Understanding Political Systems. New York: Gareth Stevens Publishing, 2014.

Sauers, Richard Allen. *Nationalism.* Key Concepts in American History. New York: Chelsea House Publishing, 2010.

Websites

www.history.com/topics/american-revolution/american-revolution-history
This website provides links to information about all aspects of the American Revolution and the influence of the Constitution

http://www.history.com/topics/ancient-history/ancient-greece-democracy
This website features information about the earliest known form of democracy in ancient Athens, Greece.

www.historyforkids.net/roman-government.html
This website discusses the different forms of Roman government under the monarchy, the republic, and the empire.

http://www.historynet.com/womens-suffrage-movement
This website features information about the Womens Suffrage Movement in Europe and the United States.

http://nationalgeographic.org/encyclopedia/globalization/
This encyclopedic entry from the National Geographic Society explains the process of globalization.

http://nehsushistory-ww2.weebly.com/lesson-3-the-rise-of-dictators.html
This online lesson features videos and a quiz about the rise of dictators in the 1920s and 1930s.

Publisher's note to educators and parents: Our editors have carefully reviewed these websites to ensure that they are suitable for students. Many websites change frequently, however, and we cannot guarantee that a site's future contents will continue to meet our high standards of quality and educational value. Be advised that students should be closely supervised whenever they access the Internet.

INDEX